GARDEN VASES

ISBN 2-909838-42-0

Andrew Zega and Bernd H. Dams

GARDEN VASES

Introduction by Gérard Mabille

ALAIN de GOURCUFF ÉDITEUR

For Hervé Aaron

On its plinth, finally, the Great Urn stood,
Naked from foot to handles in the silence,
While, spiralling around the living marble,
The scattered dance, its vanished murmurs
Echoing on the languid breeze,
Twirled goats, gods and nudes,
Rearing centaurs and graceful fauns,
Silently around the wall...

Henri de Régnier
Les Jeux rustiques et divins, 1918.

Garden Urns and Vases

Great urns and vases in marble, bronze or lead are among the most handsome ornaments of classical gardens. They are to be found in particular abundance at Versailles, where they line parterres and bosquets or punctuate avenues and perspectives with their monumental silhouettes. Lofty landmarks or guardian spirits, they seem to invite those strolling through the gardens to pause a moment to contemplate the scenes from classical mythology — the childhood of the gods, triumphal processions, sacrifices to propitiate the gods, Bacchic dances — that unfurl seamlessly on the flawless curves of their flanks.

One of the most impassioned muses of Versailles, Henri de Régnier, celebrates their beauty in *Les Jeux rustiques et divins* quoted above. There can be no mistaking the identity of this vase, carved with its 'mad pursuit' of gods and fauns, maenads and naked women: it is none other than the Borghese urn.

The prestigious urns and vases of classical architecture and gardens were inspired, indeed, by models from ancient Rome, and most particularly by the greatly admired Borghese and Medici urns. These great marble urns, named after the powerful dynasties to whom they once belonged, were the finest known examples of the chalice-shaped neo-Attic urns inspired by the metal vases characteristic of the fifth century BC. Greek in origin but discovered in sixteenth-century Rome, both are believed to date from the second half of the first century BC. The Borghese urn, decorated with a frieze in high relief depicting a Bacchic procession, was unearthed in the Gardens of Sallust in the late 1560s; in 1649, it became part of the Borghese collection in

Rome. When this collection was taken to Paris in 1808, the vase entered the collections of the Louvre, where it remains to this day. The Medici urn, meanwhile, carved with scenes depicting preparations for the Trojan war and the sacrifice of Iphigenia, was also excavated in Rome, where it remained in the collection of the Grand Dukes of Tuscany until 1780. In that year it was taken to Florence, where it may still be seen in the Uffizi Gallery.

In 1666, Louis XIV and Colbert created the French Academy in Rome, so that young French artists might imbue themselves with the perfection of classical art. For sculptors, making copies of classical Greek and Roman models thus became the foundation of an ideal training — with the added advantage that these scholarly exercises could also serve as ornaments for royal residences and gardens. A plethora of replicas of the Borghese and Medici urns thus appeared, many subsequently to be sent to Versailles. Still today, three magnificent copies of these two masterpieces of antiquity adorn the Parterre de Latone, where they were placed in 1682. But this was not to be the end of the matter. While copying was a necessary exercise, contemporary artists were equally anxious to demonstrate that their talents equalled those of the ancients, and vied with each other in creating urns and vases that rivalled or even surpassed their classical models while also exalting the glory of the king.

Thus in 1684, two great vases by Coysevox and Tubi, representing Peace and War, took their places beneath the palace walls. Continuing the themes of the two salons of the Grande Galerie, they celebrated respectively France's dominion over Spain and her defeat of the Turks in Hungary, and the peace treaties of Nijmegen and Aix-la-Chapelle. In their outlines and

———————

their high-relief friezes, both were brilliant transpositions of antique models. To the west, meanwhile, overlooking Latonus from the far end of the Parterre d'Eau, a pair of urns carved with masks of radiant suns crowned with laurel wreaths, by Drouilly and Dugoulon (1684-9), exalted the omnipresent myth of Apollo the sun god. Lower down, another pair, by Hardy and Prou (1688), recalled Louis XIV's victories over the Empire and Spain, symbolized by a throng of chubby-cheeked cherubs playing with the attributes of Mars. Further on, along the Allée Royale, seven pairs of great marble urns punctuate the majestic descent to the Bassin d'Apollon. Executed after 1685, they represented a new stylistic development, as narratives in bas-relief gave way to purely decorative elements — arabesques, flower garlands, foliage and cornucopias — combined with royal and solar emblems. The beauty of these pieces now derived solely from the supreme and unadorned elegance of their lines.

While marble was the medium par excellence of the most monumental urns and vases at Versailles, metal was also a favoured material; more than any others, vases in precious metal were the most appropriate symbol of a return to a Golden Age. Beginning in 1666, Le Brun designed a set of fourteen silver urns intended to hold orange trees in the royal apartments. Executed by the most accomplished silversmiths in the kingdom — Ballin, Loir, Dutel and Cousinet — these great vessels (standing nearly a metre tall and weighing some 80 kilograms each) were all variations on the Borghese and Medici models. With their highly varied decorative themes inspired by classical mythology, they celebrated the newly rediscovered gods and legends of antiquity. When the palace was later enlarged by Le Vau, they were installed in the great apartments, only to be abruptly removed and melted down — along with most of the other silver in the palace — in 1690. However, a valuable reflection of them survives in the gardens at the foot of the palace walls, in the form of the celebrated set of twenty-six bronze vases attributed to Ballin, some of which are illustrated in this volume. What do these masterpieces owe to the great goldsmith Ballin? No one knows for certain, though some speculate that he produced the designs. What we do know is that the models were supplied from 1665 by the sculptors Anguier, Magnier, Legendre and Tubi, and that the finished pieces were cast by Duval, Prévost and Picard. Arranged in pairs on the marble sills overlooking the Parterre du Nord and the Parterre du Midi, the 'Ballin' vases display imagination and poetry in equal measure in their interpretation of classical Greek and Roman sources. Decorated with antique medallions, gadroons, ova and frets, and garlands of laurel and oak, acanthus and ivy, they are enlivened by a throng of playful or pouting cupids, chimeras, sphinxes, dragons and satyrs, while Apollo is depicted in pursuit of Daphne or slaying the serpent Python (see pp. 17, 27 and 103). Of remarkably skilful workmanship, they were doubtless intended to be gilded, though this work was never carried out. Like their silver counterparts, they are imbued with a lyricism that is at once subtle, harmonious and consummately Virgilian in spirit, offering a wealth of variations upon the most appealing aspects of classical mythology — hunting, love and dionysian intoxication — mingled with an exquisite sensitivity to nature, life and youthful beauty, radiant and eternal.

Other parts of the garden were also furnished with urns fashioned of metal. Gilt lead was chosen for the equally spectacular though less-precious ensembles that graced the great Bassin de Neptune and several of the more distant bosquets, such as the Salle de Bal, for this was the realm of illusion. Friezes on the urns in the Salle de Bal, carved in 1682 by Le Hongre, Le Gros and Jouvenet, depicted dancing nymphs. The seven pairs arranged around the Bassin de Neptune, created in the same year by a large team including Coysevox, Raon, Cornu and Prou, were less Attic and more baroque in inspiration; at times grotesque, at times fantastical, they exhibit an astonishing degree of vitality. With their distorted forms and decorative details — featuring crayfish, lizards, dragons, tritons and other sea monsters — they evoke the disturbing watery realm of Neptune (see pp. 21, 23 and 99).

Nor was Versailles the only great French garden to boast quantities of urns and vases. At Marly, Louis XIV's fabled estate, they appeared in even greater numbers, in marble or lead, adorning steps, terraces and parterres (see p. 19). But it was at La Granja, laid out by Philip V of Spain from 1720 (and doubtless inspired by his childhood memories as a prince of the French royal family), that garden urns and vases were to reach their true apogee. Here the Versailles-trained sculptors Thierry, Frémin and Bousseau placed them in their hundreds along parterres and avenues and around fountains and basins; cast and sculpted in lead and painted white in imitation of marble, to this day they embody the triumph of the rococo and the baroque in the last gardens à la française ever to be created by a Bourbon king.

« Sir, I hate urns! Would they were beaten to pieces to pave our streets! »

Dr. Samuel Johnson

Bronze urn with sphinxes
Design attributed to Claude Ballin
for the Parterre du Midi at Versailles
1665

Lead ewer with dragon handle
Executed by Jean Hardy
for the Cascade Champêtre at Marly
1706

Gilt lead urn
Design attributed to Charles Le Brun
for the Bassin de Neptune at Versailles
1682

Lead urn with crayfish handles
Design attributed to Charles Le Brun
for the Bassin de Neptune at Versailles
1682

Gritstone vase
Design by Jeffrey Wyattville
Chatsworth, Derbyshire
*c.*1820

Bronze urn with cupids
Design attributed to Claude Ballin
Parterre du Nord, Versailles
1665

White marble neo-classical urn
Design by Joseph Magg
Germany
*c.*1780

Sandstone vase and plinth
Design attributed to Daniel Harvey
Castle Howard, Yorkshire
Early eighteenth century

Neo-classical urn in pink sandstone
Wilton House, Wiltshire
Late eighteenth century

Stone flower basket
Design by Jacques-François Blondel
1737

Stone vase in the Mannerist style
Montacute House, Somerset
Early seventeenth century

White marble vase with rams' heads
Design by Ennemond Alexandre Petitot
Executed for the gardens of
the Duke of Parma
1756

Sandstone urn with garlands
Château de Belœil, Belgium
Late eighteenth century

Limestone urn and console
Pitzhanger Manor, Ealing
Late eighteenth century

Bronze urn
Design attributed to Claude Ballin
for the parterres at Versailles
1665

Lead vase with flower garlands
Design attributed to Lord Burlington
Chiswick House, London
Mid-eighteenth century

Portland stone vase
Design attributed to Grinling Gibbons
Syon House, Middlesex
*c.*1700

Limestone *cassolette*
Désert de Retz, Chambourcy
Late eighteenth century

Lead urn
Powis Castle, Powys, Wales
Early eighteenth century

Limestone finial
England
Early seventeenth century

Urn with flaming finial
Design by Sir John Vanbrugh
Blenheim Palace, Oxfordshire
*c.*1715

Limestone urn
Hampstead Marshal, Berkshire
Late eighteenth century

Vase in Languedoc marble
Design by the atelier of Charles Nizet
for the Château de Raray, Oise
Early twentieth century

Bath stone urn
Design attributed to William Kent
Rousham, Oxfordshire
*c.*1740

Limestone vase
After a design by Lord Burlington
Petworth House, West Sussex
Mid-eighteenth century

Portland stone fruit basket
on a baluster base
Castle Howard, Yorkshire
Early eighteenth century

Neo-classical Coade stone vase
Coade Manufactory, England
*c.*1800

Terracotta urn
England
Mid-nineteenth century

Limestone urn
Vine House, Kingston
Late seventeenth century

Limestone urn
After a design by William Kent
Notgrove Manor, Gloucestershire
Mid-eighteenth century

Pink marble vase
Design by the atelier of Charles Nizet
for the Château de Raray, Oise
Early twentieth century

White marble urn with battle scene
Design by Charles Le Brun
for the gardens at Versailles
*c.*1678

Limestone finial
Bowood House, Wiltshire
Late eighteenth century

Neo-classical Bath stone vase
Design by William Kent
Chiswick House, London
1735

Limestone flaming finial
Design by Jules Hardouin-Mansart
for the Grand Trianon at Versailles
1687

Terracotta urn
Cast by James Blashfield
Royal Botanic Gardens, Kew, London
*c.*1865

Bronze urn with lions' heads
Design attributed to Claude Ballin
Parterre du Nord, Versailles
1665

Terracotta covered urn
Executed for the gardens at Marly
*c.*1700

Lead urn with lobsters
Design by Jean-Jacques Clérion
for the Bassin de Neptune at Versailles
*c.*1683

Stone flower basket
Design by the atelier of
Jules Hardouin-Mansart
Grand Trianon, Versailles
1687

Whitewashed terracotta vase
Orangery, Bowood House, Wiltshire
Mid-nineteenth century

Neo-classical white marble urn
Design by the atelier of
Jules Hardouin-Mansart
Parterre du Nord, Versailles
*c.*1687

Bronze urn with scroll handles
Design by François Anguier
Parterre du Nord, Versailles
*c.*1665

Lead urn with snake handles
Design attributed to Charles Le Brun
Bassin de Neptune, Versailles
1683

Limestone vase with festoons
Brympton Manor, Somerset
Late seventeenth century

Enamelled metal urn
Designed for the Porcelain Trianon
at Versailles
c.1674

Printed in 2000
for ALAIN de GOURCUFF ÉDITEUR

Designed by Maxence Scherf

Phototypeset, photogravure and printing by
Imprimerie Escourbiac, Graulhet (Tarn), France